THE "MONITOR."   THE "MERRIMAC."

THE ENCOUNTER AT SHORT RANGE.

THE MONITOR
AND
THE MERRIMAC

BOTH SIDES OF THE STORY

TOLD BY

LIEUT. J. L. WORDEN, U.S.N.

LIEUT. GREENE, U.S.N.

Of THE MONITOR
AND

H. ASHTON RAMSAY, C.S.N.

CHIEF ENGINEER OP THE MERRIMAC

ILLUSTRATED

HARPER & BROTHERS PUBLISHERS

NEW YORK AND LONDON

MCMXII

THE MONITOR

AND

THE MERRIMAC

TOLD BY

LIEUT. J. L. WORDEN, U.S.N.
LIEUT. GREENE, U.S.N.

OF THE MONITOR

AND

H. ASHTON RAMSAY, C.S.N.

CHIEF ENGINEER OF THE MERRIMAC

Digital Scanning and Publishing is a leader in the electronic republication of historical books and documents. We publish many of our titles as eBooks, paperback and hardcover editions. DSI is committed to bringing many traditional and well-known books back to life, retaining the look and feel of the original work.

Trade Paperback ISBN: 1-58218-836-X

©2009 DSI Digital Reproduction
First DSI Printing: December 2009

Published by Digital Scanning Inc. Scituate, MA 02066
781-545-2100 http://www.Digitalscanning.com and
http://www.PDFLibrary.com

CONTENTS

CONFEDERATE BATTERY, SEWELL'S POINT.   CONFEDERATE BATTERY, CRANEY ISLAND   CONFEDERATE BATTERIES AT PIG POINT AND BARREL POINT.   JAMES RIVER.

CONFEDERATE STEAMERS "YORKTOWN" AND "JAMESTOWN."

GOSPORT   UNION BATTERY RIP-RAPS.   FRENCH MAN-OF-WAR.   "MONITOR" AND "MERRIMAC."   "MINNESOTA."   FORT MONROE   WRECKS OF "CONGRESS" AND "CUMBERLAND"

PORTSMOUTH.   U. S. FRIGATE "ROANOKE" AND TRANSPORTS AND STORE SHIPS.   UNION BATTERIES AND CAMP AT NEWPOET NEWS-

NORFOLK.   HAMPTON

BIRD'S-EYE VIEW OF THE ENGAGEMENT BETWEEN THE "MONITOR" AND THE "MERRIMAC."

INTRODUCTION

THIS is the first-hand story of what was done and seen and felt on each side in the battle of the *Monitor* and the *Merrimac.* The actual experiences on both vessels are pictured, in one case by the commander of the *Monitor,* then a lieutenant, and the next in rank, Lieutenant Greene, and in the other by Chief-Engineer Ramsay of the *Merrimac.* Clearly such a record of personal experiences has a place by itself in the literature of the subject.

It is quite unnecessary to dwell upon the various controversies which

INTRODUCTION

this battle has involved. As to the first use of armor, we know that France experimented with floating armored batteries in the Crimean War, and England had armored ships before 1862. As to the invention of the movable turret, which has been a bone of contention, the pages of Colonel Church's *Life of John Ericsson* and other books are open to the curious. The struggle of Ericsson to obtain official recognition, the raising of money, the hasty equipment of the *Monitor,* and the restraining orders under which she fought form a story supplementary to the battle, but of peculiar interest. The *Monitor* was ordered to act on the defensive. It was her mission first to protect the wooden ships. That explains certain misconceptions of her

INTRODUCTION

cautious attitude. And the fact that the powder charges for her Dahlgren guns were officially limited to fifteen pounds, although thirty and even fifty pounds were used with safety afterward, invites speculation upon the results if she had fought with a free hand.

But the main result was reached. The Union fleet was saved. The career of the *Merrimac* was checked. No Union vessel was destroyed after the *Monitor* appeared. It seems proper to note these facts here, in view of the fact that Mr. Ramsay's fresh and striking story of the *Merrimac*, which is presented for the first time, enters upon the details of the battle more fully than the narrative of Lieutenant Worden and Lieutenant Greene. Fortunately the discussion has become academic in the half-century

INTRODUCTION

that has passed since Southern cheers over the first conquests of the *Merrimac* faltered before the acclaim which greeted the *Monitors* achievement of her task. One may disagree with the phrasing of various historians on both sides, one may find it difficult to accept the inscription upon the shaft of the *Merrimac* outside the "Confederate White House" in Richmond, but no American can cease to wonder at the fortitude and daring of those other Americans who fought to the death in those hastily improvised crafts, bearing the brunt not only of battle, but of a strange and terrible experiment. It is not an argument that this book offers, but a saga of heroes, an illumination of qualities which have made our history in times of crisis.

INTRODUCTION

The year of this battle witnessed the destruction of both the vessels engaged. Mr. Ramsay describes the blowing - up of the *Merrimac.* An eye - witness of the sinking of the *Monitor* off Hatteras, Rear-Admiral E. W. Watson, who was an officer of the *Rhode Island,* which was towing the *Monitor* on that eventful night, has very kindly written a brief description of the tragedy for this book.

The publishers desire to make acknowledgment to the representatives of the late Lucius E. Chittenden for the use of Part I of this book, which appears in Mr. Chittenden's most interesting volume, *Recollections of President Lincoln and his Administration.*

THE MONITOR AND THE MERRIMAC

THE MONITOR AND THE MERRIMAC

I

Told by Lieutenant Worden and Lieutenant S. D. Greene
of the "Monitor"

SOME weeks after the historic battle between the Monitor and the Merrimac in Hampton Roads, on March 9, 1862, the former vessel came to the Washington Navy-yard unchanged, in the same condition as when she discharged her parting shot at the Merrimac. There she lay until her heroic commander had so far recovered from his injuries as to be able to rejoin his vessel. All leaves of absence had been revoked, the absentees had returned, and were ready to welcome their captain. President Lincoln, Captain Fox, and a limited number of Captain Worden's personal friends had been invited to his informal reception. Lieutenant Greene received the President and the guests. He was a boy in years—not too young to volunteer, however, when volunteers were scarce, and to fight the *Merrimac* during the last half of the battle, after the captain was disabled.

The President and the other guests stood on the deck, near the turret. The men were formed in lines, with their officers a little in advance, when Captain Worden ascended the gangway. The heavy guns in the navy-yard began firing the customary sa-

THE MONITOR AND THE MERRIMAC

lute when he stepped upon the deck. One side of his face was permanently blackened by the powder shot into it from the muzzle of a cannon carrying a shell of one hundred pounds' weight, discharged less than twenty yards away. The President advanced to welcome him, and introduced him to the few strangers present. The officers and men passed in review and were dismissed. Then there was a scene worth witnessing. The old tars swarmed around their loved captain, they grasped his hand, crowded to touch him, thanked God for his recovery and return, and invoked blessings upon his head in the name of all the saints in the calendar. He called them by their names, had a pleasant word for each of them, and for a few moments we looked upon

3

an exhibition of a species of affection that could only have been the product of a common danger.

When order was restored, the President gave a brief sketch of Captain Worden's career. Commodore Paulding had been the first, Captain Worden the second officer, of the navy, he said, to give an unqualified opinion in favor of armored vessels. Their opinions had been influential with him and with the Board of Construction. Captain Worden had volunteered to take command of the *Monitor*, at the risk of his life and reputation, before the keel was laid! He had watched her construction, and his energy had made it possible to send her to sea in time to arrest the destructive operations of the *Merrimac*. What he had done with a new crew, and a vessel of novel construction, we all knew. He, the President, cordially acknowledged his indebtedness to Captain Worden, and he hoped the whole country would unite in the feeling of obligation. The debt was a heavy one, and would not be repudiated when its nature was understood. The details of the first battle between ironclads would interest every one. At the request of Captain Fox, Captain Worden had consented to give an account of his voyage from New York to Hampton Roads, and of what had afterward happened there on board the *Monitor*.

In an easy conversational manner, without any effort at display, Captain Worden told the story, of which the following is the substance:

"I suppose," he began, "that every one knows that we left New York

Harbor in some haste. We had information that the *Merrimac* was nearly completed, and if we were to fight her on her first appearance, we must be on the ground. The *Monitor* had been hurried from the laying of her keel. Her engines were new, and her machinery did not move smoothly. Never was a vessel launched that so much needed trial-trips to test her machinery and get her crew accustomed to their novel duties. We went to sea practically without them. No part of the vessel was finished; there was one omission that was serious, and came very near causing her failure and the loss of many lives. In heavy weather it was intended that her hatches and all her openings should be closed and battened down. In that case all the men would be below, and would have to depend upon artificial ventilation. Our machinery for that purpose proved wholly inadequate.

"We were in a heavy gale of wind as soon as we passed Sandy Hook. The vessel behaved splendidly. The seas rolled over her, and we found her the most comfortable vessel we had ever seen, except for the ventilation, which gave us more trouble than I have time to tell you about. We had to run into port and anchor on account of the weather, and, as you know, it was two o'clock in the morning of Sunday before we were alongside the *Minnesota*. Captain Van Brunt gave us an account of Saturday's experience. He was very glad to make our acquaintance, and notified us that we must be prepared to receive the *Merrimac* at daylight. We had had a very hard trip down the coast, and officers and men were weary and sleepy. But when informed that our fight would probably open at daylight, and that the *Monitor* must be put in order, every man went to his post with a cheer. That night there was no sleep on board the *Monitor.*

"In the gray of the early morning we saw a vessel approaching, which our friends on the *Minnesota* said was the *Merrimac.* Our fastenings were cast off, our machinery started, and we moved out to meet her half-way. We had come a long way to fight her, and did not intend to lose our opportunity.

"Before showing you over the vessel, let me say that there were three possible points of weakness in the

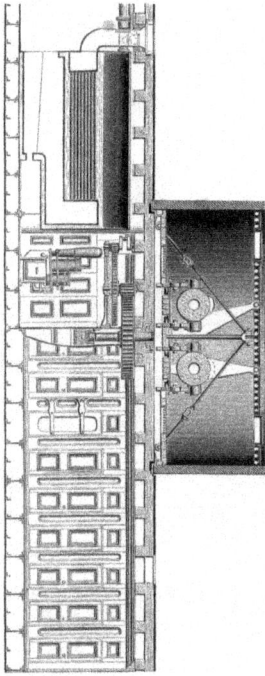

2. CENTRAL SECTION

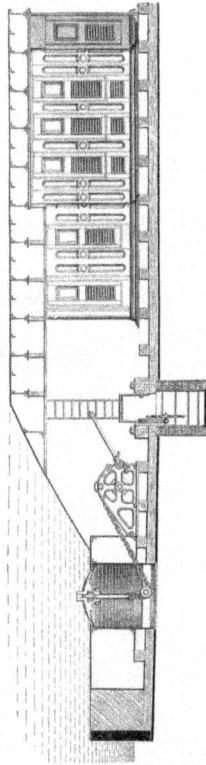

3. FORWARD SECTION.

TRANSVERSE SECTION OF THE "MONITOR" THROUGHT
THE CENTER OF THE TURRET.

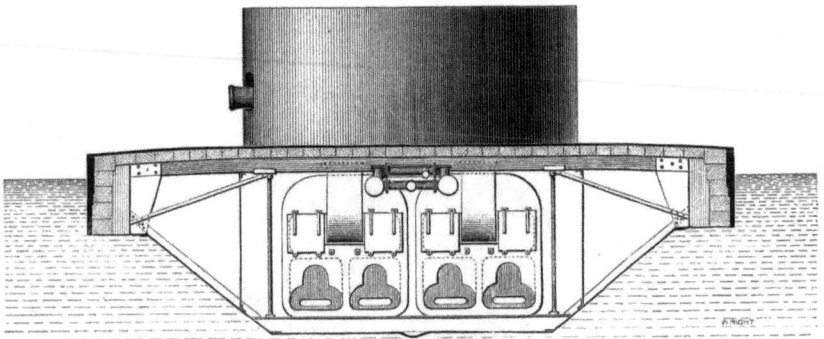

TRANSVERSE SECTION OF THE HULL OF THE ORIGINAL MONITOR.

THE MONITOR AND THE MERRIMAC

Monitor, two of which might have been guarded against in her construction, if there had been more time to perfect her plans. One of them was in the turret, which, as you see, is constructed of eight plates of inch iron—on the side of the ports, nine— set on end so as to break joints, and firmly bolted together, making a hollow cylinder eight inches thick. It rests on a metal ring on a vertical shaft, which is revolved by power from the boilers. If a projectile struck the turret at an acute angle, it was expected to glance off without doing damage. But what would happen if it was fired in a straight line to the center of the turret, which in that case would receive the whole force of the blow? It might break off the bolt-heads on the interior, which, flying across, would kill the men at the guns; it might disarrange the revolving mechanism, and then we would be wholly disabled.

"I laid the *Monitor* close alongside the *Merrimac,* and gave her a shot. She returned our compliment by a shell weighing one hundred and fifty pounds, fired when we were close together, which struck the turret so squarely that it received the whole force. Here you see the scar, two and a half inches deep in the wrought iron, a perfect mold of the shell. If anything could test the turret, it was that shot. It did not start a rivet-head or a nut! It stunned the two men who were nearest where the ball struck, and that was all. I touched the lever —the turret revolved as smoothly as before. The turret had stood the

VIEW SHOWING THE EFFECT OF SHOT ON THE "MONITOR" TURRET.

THE "MONITOR" IN BATTLE TRIM.

test; I could mark that point of weakness off my list forever.

"You notice that the deck is joined to the side of the hull by a right angle, at what sailors call the 'plank-shear.' If a projectile struck that angle what would happen? It would not be deflected; its whole force would be expended there. It might open a seam in the hull below the water-line, or pierce the wooden hull, and sink us. Here was our second point of weakness.

"I had decided how I would fight her in advance. I would keep the *Monitor* moving in a circle just large enough to give time for loading the guns. At the point where the circle impinged upon the *Merrimac* our guns should be fired, and loaded while we were moving around the circuit. Evidently the *Merrimac* would return the compliment every time. At our second exchange of shots, she returning six or eight to our two, another of her large shells struck our 'plank-shear' at its angle, and tore up one of the deck-plates, as you see. The shell had struck what I believed to be the weakest point in the *Monitor*. We had already learned that the *Merrimac* swarmed with sharpshooters, for their bullets were constantly spattering against our turret and our deck. If a man showed himself on deck he would draw their fire. But I did not much consider the sharpshooters. It was my duty to investigate the effects of that shot. I ordered one of the pendulums to be hauled aside, and, crawling out of the port, walked to the side, lay down upon my chest, and

JOHN L. WORDEN, REAR-ADMIRAL, U. S. N.
Commander of the "Monitor" in the engagement with the "Merrimac."
From a photograph taken in 1875.

IN THE TURRET OF THE "MONITOR."

examined it thoroughly. The hull was uninjured, except for a few splinters in the wood. I walked back and crawled into the turret—the bullets were falling on the iron deck all about me as thick as hail-stones in a storm. None struck me, I suppose because the vessel was moving, and at the angle, and when I was lying on the deck my body made a small mark, difficult to hit. We gave them two more guns, and then I told the men, what was true, that the *Merrimac* could not sink us if we let her pound us for a month. The men cheered; the knowledge put new life into all.

"We had more exchanges, and then the *Merrimac* tried new tactics. She endeavored to ram us, to run us down. Once she struck us about amidships with her iron ram. Here you see its

13

mark. It gave us a shock, pushed us around, and that was all the harm. But the movement placed our sides together. I gave her two guns, which I think lodged in her side, for, from my lookout crack, I could not see that either shot rebounded. Ours being the smaller vessel, and more easily handled, I had no difficulty in avoiding her ram. I ran around her several times, planting our shot in what seemed to be the most vulnerable places. In this way, reserving my fire until I got the range and the mark, I planted two more shots almost in the very spot I had hit when she tried to ram us. Those shots must have been effective, for they were followed by a shower of bars of iron.

"The third weak spot was our pilot-house. You see that it is built

THE MONITOR AND THE MERRIMAC

a little more than three feet above the deck, of bars of iron, ten by twelve inches square, built up like a log-house, bolted with very large bolts at the corners where the bars interlock. The pilot stands upon a platform below, his head and shoulders in the pilot-house. The upper tier of bars is separated from the second by an open space of an inch, through which the pilot may look out at every point of the compass. The pilot-house, as you see, is a foursquare mass of iron, provided with no means of deflecting a ball. I expected trouble from it, and I was not disappointed. Until my accident happened, as we approached the enemy I stood in the pilot-house and gave the signals. Lieutenant Greene fired the guns, and Engineer Stimers, here, revolved the turret.

THE MONITOR AND THE MERRIMAC

"I was below the deck when the corner of the pilot-house was first struck by a shot or a shell. It either burst or was broken, and no harm was done. A short time after I had given the signal and, with my eye close against the lookout crack, was watching the effect of our shot, something happened to me —my part in the fight was ended. Lieutenant Greene, who fought the *Merrimac* until she had no longer stomach for fighting, will tell you the rest of the story."

Can it be possible that this beardless boy fought one of the historic battles of the world? This was the thought of every one, as the modest, diffident young Greene was half pushed forward into the circle.

"I cannot add much to the Captain's story," he began. " He had cut

THE MONITOR AND THE MERRIMAC

out the work for us, and we had only to follow his pattern. I kept the *Monitor* either moving around the circle or around the enemy, and endeavored to place our shots as near her amidships as possible, where Captain Worden believed he had already broken through her armor. We knew that she could not sink us, and I thought I would keep right on pounding her as long as she would stand it. There is really nothing new to be added to Captain Worden's account. We could strike her wherever we chose. Weary as they must have been, our men were full of enthusiasm, and I do not think we wasted a shot. Once we ran out of the circle for a moment to adjust a piece of machinery, and I learn that some of our friends feared that we were drawing out of the fight.

THE MONITOR AND THE MERRIMAC

The *Merrimac* took the opportunity to start for Norfolk. As soon as our machinery was adjusted we followed her, and got near enough to give her a parting shot. But I was not familiar with the locality; there might be torpedoes planted in the channel, and I did not wish to take any risk of losing our vessel, so I came back to the company of our friends. But except that we were, all of us, tired and hungry when we came back to the *Minnesota* at half-past twelve P.M., the *Monitor* was just as well prepared to fight as she was at eight o'clock in the morning when she fired the first gun."

We were then shown the injury to the pilot-house. The mark of the ball was plain upon the two upper bars, the principal impact being upon the lower of the two. This huge bar

THE MONITOR AND THE MERRIMAC

was broken in the middle, but held firmly at either end. The farther it was pressed in, the stronger was the resistance on the exterior. On the inside the fracture in the bar was half an inch wide. Captain Worden's eye was very near to the lookout crack, so that when the gun was discharged the shock of the ball knocked him senseless, while the mass of flame filled one side of his face with coarse grains of powder. He remained insensible for some hours.

"Have you heard what Captain Worden's first inquiry was when he recovered his senses after the general shock to his system?" asked Captain Fox of the President.

"I think I have," replied Mr. Lincoln, "but it is worth relating to these gentlemen."

THE MONITOR AND THE MERRIMAC

"His question was," said Captain Fox, "'Have I saved the *Minnesota?'*

"'Yes, and whipped the *Merrimac!'* some one answered.

"'Then,' said Captain Worden, 'I don't care what becomes of me.'

"Mr. President," said Captain Fox, "not much of the history to which we have listened is new to me. I saw this battle from eight o'clock until midday. There was one marvel in it which has not been mentioned—the splendid handling of the *Monitor* throughout the battle. The first bold advance of this diminutive vessel against a gaint like the *Merrimac* was superlatively grand. She seemed inspired by Nelson's order at Trafalgar: 'He will make no mistake who lays

20

THE MONITOR AND THE MERRIMAC

his vessel alongside the enemy.' One would have thought the *Monitor* a living thing. No man was visible. You saw her moving around that circle, delivering her fire invariably at the point of contact, and heard the crash of the missile against her enemy's armor above the thunder of her guns, on the bank where we stood. It was indescribably grand!

"Now," he continued, "standing here on the deck of this battle-scarred vessel, the first genuine ironclad—the victor in the first fight of the iron-clads—let me make a confession and perform an act of simple justice: I never fully believed in armored vessels until I saw this battle. I know all the facts which united to give us the *Monitor*. I withhold no credit from Captain Ericsson, her inventor, but

THE MONITOR AND THE MERRIMAC

I know that the country is principally indebted for the construction of this vessel to President Lincoln, and for the success of her trial to Captain Worden, her commander."

THE MERRIMAC AND THE MONITOR

II
THE MERRIMAC AND THE MONITOR

Told by H. Ashton Ramsay, Major C. S. A., Chief Engineer of the "Merrimac"

THE *Merrimac* was built in 1856 as a full-rigged war-frigate, of thirty-one hundred tons' burden, with auxiliary steam power to be used only in case of head winds. She was a hybrid from her birth, marking the transition from sails to steam as well as from wooden ships to ironclads.

I became her second assistant engineer in Panama Bay in 1859, cruising in her around the Horn and back

THE MERRIMAC AND THE MONITOR

to Norfolk. Her chief engineer was Alban C. Stimers. Little did we dream that he was to be the right-hand man of Ericsson in the construction of the *Monitor*, while I was to hold a similar post in the conversion of our own ship into an ironclad, or that, in less than a year and a half, we would be seeking to destroy each other, he as chief engineer of the *Monitor* and I in the corresponding position on the *Merrimac*.

In the harbor of Rio on our return voyage we met the *Congress*, and as we sailed away after coaling she fired a friendly salute and cheered us, and we responded with a will. When the two ships next met it was in one of the deadliest combats of naval history.

The machinery of the *Merrimac* was condemned, and she went out of com-

THE UNITED STATES FRIGATE "MERRIMAC"

Before and after conversion into an iron-clad.

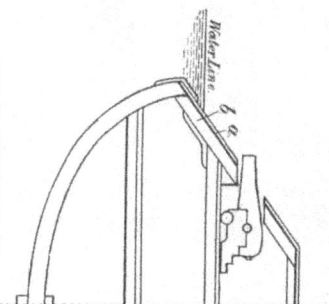

CROSS-SECTION OF "MERRIMAC."

From a drawing by John L. Porter, Constructor.

a — 4 inches of iron.

b — 22 inches of wood.

Water Line

THE BURNING OF THE FRIGATE "MERRIMAC" AND OF THE GOSPORT NAVY YARD

mission on our return. She was still at Norfolk when the war broke out, and was set on fire by the Federals when Norfolk was evacuated. Some of the workmen in the navy-yard scuttled and sank her, thus putting out the flames. When she was raised by the Confederates she was nothing but a burned and blackened hulk.

Her charred upper works were cut away, and in the center a casement shield one hundred and eighty feet long was built of pitch-pine and oak, two feet thick. This was covered with iron plates, one to two inches thick and eight inches wide, bolted over each other and through and through the woodwork, giving a protective armor four inches in thickness. The shield sloped at an angle of about thirty-six degrees, and was covered

3

with an iron grating that served as an upper deck.
For fifty feet forward and aft her decks were submerged below the water, and the prow was shod
with an iron beak to receive the impact when
ramming.

Even naval officers were skeptical as to the result.
The plates were rolled at the Tredegar mills at
Richmond, and arrived so slowly that we were nearly
a year in finishing her. We could have rolled them at
Norfolk and built four *Merrimacs* in that time, had
the South understood the importance of a navy at
the outbreak of the war.

I remember that my old friend and comrade,
Captain Charles MacIntosh, while awaiting orders,
used to come over and stand on the granite curbing
of the dock to watch the work as it crawled along.

REMODELING
THE "MERRIMAC"
At the Gosport Navy Yard.

THE "MERRIMAC" PASSING THE CONFEDERATE BATTERY ON CRANEY ISLAND , ON
HER WAY TO ATTACK THE FEDERAL FLEET.

THE MERRIMAC AND THE MONITOR

"Good-by, Ramsay," he said, sadly, on the eve of starting to command a ram at New Orleans. "I shall never see you again. She will prove your coffin." A short time afterward the poor fellow had both legs shot from under him and died almost immediately.

Rifled guns were just coming into use, and Lieutenant Brooke, who designed the *Merrimac,* considered the question of having some of her guns rifled. How to procure such cannon was not easily discovered, as we had no foundries in the South. There were many cast-iron cannon that had fallen into our hands at Norfolk, and he conceived the idea of turning some of this ordnance into rifles. In order to enable them to stand the additional bursting strain we forged wrought-iron bands and shrank them over the chambers, and we devised a special tool for rifling the bore of the guns. They gave effective service.

Many details remained uncompleted when we were at last floated out of dry-dock, but there was great pressure for us to make some demonstration that might serve to check McClellan in his advance up the Peninsula.

The ship was still full of workmen hurrying her to completion when Commodore Franklin Buchanan arrived from Richmond one March morning and ordered every one out of the ship, except her crew of three hundred and fifty men which had been hastily drilled on shore in the management of the big guns, and directed Executive Officer Jones to prepare to sail at once.

At that time nothing was known of

our destination. All we knew was that we were off at last. Buchanan sent for me. The veteran sailor, the beau ideal of a naval officer of the old school, with his tall form, harsh features, and clear, piercing eyes, was pacing the deck with a stride I found it difficult to match, although he was then over sixty and I but twenty-four.

"Ramsay," he asked, "what would happen to your engines and boilers if there should be a collision?"

"They are braced tight," I assured him. " Though the boilers stand fourteen feet, they are so securely fastened that no collision could budge them."

"I am going to ram the *Cumberland,*" said my commander. "I'm told she has the new rifled guns, the only ones in their whole fleet we have cause to fear. The moment we are

31

in the Roads I'm going to make right for her and ram her. How about your engines? They were in bad shape in the old ship, I understand. Can we rely on them? Should they be tested by a trial trip?"

"She will have to travel some ten miles down the river before we get to the Roads," I said. "If any trouble develops I'll report it. I think that will be sufficient trial trip."

I watched the machinery carefully as we sped down the Elizabeth River, and soon satisfied myself that all was well. Then I went on deck.

"How fast is she going do you think?" I asked one of the pilots.

"Eight or nine knots an hour," he replied, making a rapid calculation from objects ashore. The *Merrimac* as an ironclad was faster under steam than she had ever been before with her top hamper of masts and sails.

I presented myself to the commodore. "The machinery is all right, sir," I assured him.

Across the river at Newport News gleamed the batteries and white tents of the Federal camp and the vessels of the fleet blockading the mouth of the James, chief among them the *Congress* and the *Cumberland,* tall and stately, with every line and spar clearly denned against the blue March sky, their decks and ports bristling with guns, while the rigging of the *Cumberland* was gay with the red, white, and blue of sailors' garments hung out to dry.

As we rounded into view the white-winged sailing craft that sprinkled the bay and long lines of tugs and small boats scurried to the far shore like chickens on the approach of a hovering hawk. They had seen our black hulk which looked like the roof of a barn afloat. Suddenly huge volumes of smoke began to pour from the funnels of the frigates *Minnesota* and *Roanoke* at Old Point. They had seen us, too, and were getting up steam. Bright - colored signal flags were run up and down the masts of all the ships of the Federal fleet. The *Congress* shook out her topsails. Down came the clothes-line on the *Cumberland,* and boats were lowered and dropped astern.

Our crew was summoned to the gun-deck, and Buchanan addressed us: "Sailors, in a few minutes you will have the long-looked-for opportunity of showing your devotion to our cause. Remember that you are about to strike for your country and your homes. The Confederacy expects every man to do his duty. Beat to quarters." Every terse, burning word is engraved on my memory, though fifty years have passed since they were spoken.

Just as he had finished, the mess caterer touched my elbow and whispered: "Better get your lunch now, Mr. Ramsay. It will be your last chance. The galley-fires must be put out when the magazines are opened."

On my way I saw Assistant-Surgeon Garnett at a table laying out lint and surgical implements. I had no appetite, and merely tasted some cold tongue and a cup of coffee. Passing along the gun-deck, I saw the pale and determined countenances of the guns' crews, as they stood motionless at their posts, with set lips unsmiling, contrasting with the careless expression of sailors when practised at "fighting quarters" on a man-of-war. This was the real thing.

As we approached the Federal ships we were met by a veritable storm of shells which must have sunk any ship then afloat—except the *Merrimac.* They struck our sloping sides, were deflected upward to burst harmlessly in the air, or rolled down and fell hissing into the water, dashing the spray up into our ports.

As we drew nearer the *Cumberland,* above the roar of battle rang the voice of Buchanan, "Do you surrender?"

"Never!" retorted the gallant Morris.

LIEUTENANT GEORGE U. MORRIS, U.S.N.*
Acting Commander of the "Cumberland."

THE "MERRIMAC"

From a sketch made the day before the fight.

Lt. B. L. Blackford, del. March 7, 1862

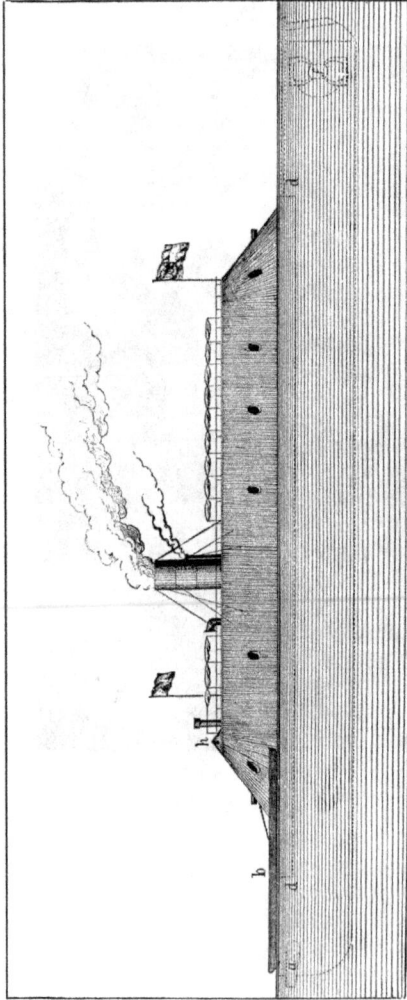

a prow, of steel
b wooden bulwark
h pilot-house

d d iron under water
f propeller

THE MERRIMAC AND THE MONITOR

The crux of what followed was down in the engine-room. Two gongs, the signal to stop, were quickly followed by three, the signal to reverse. There was an ominous pause, then a crash, shaking us all off our feet. The engines labored. The vessel was shaken in every fiber. Our bow was visibly depressed. We seemed to be bearing down with a weight on our prow. Thud, thud, thud, came the rain of shot on our shield from the double-decked battery of the *Congress.* There was a terrible crash in the fire-room. For a moment we thought one of the boilers had burst. No, it was the explosion of a shell in our stack. Was any one hit? No, thank God! The firemen had been warned to keep away from the up-take, so the fragments of shell fell harmlessly on the iron   floor-plates.

37

THE MERRIMAC AND THE MONITOR

We had rushed on the doomed ship, relentless as fate, crashing through her barricade of heavy spars and torpedo fenders, striking her below her starboard fore-chains, and crushing far into her. For a moment the whole weight of her hung on our prow and threatened to carry us down with her, the return wave of the collision curling up into our bow port.

The *Cumberland* began to sink slowly, bow first, but continued to fight desperately for the forty minutes that elapsed after her doom was sealed, while we were engaged with both the *Cumberland* and the *Congress,* being right between them.

We had left our cast-iron beak in the side of the *Cumberland.* Like the wasp, we could sting but once, leaving it in the wound.

THE "MERRIMAC" RAMMING THE "CUMBERLAND."

THE MERRIMAC AND THE MONITOR

Our smoke-stack was riddled, our flag was shot down several times, and was finally secured to a rent in the stack. On our gun-deck the men were fighting like demons. There was no thought or time for the wounded and dying as they tugged away at their guns, training and sighting their pieces while the orders rang out, "Sponge, load, fire!"

"The muzzle of our gun has been shot away," cried one of the gunners.

"No matter, keep on loading and firing—do the best you can with it," replied Lieutenant Jones.

"Keep away from the side ports, don't lean against the shield, look out for the sharpshooters," rang the warnings. Some of our men who failed to heed them and leaned against the shield were stunned and carried below, bleeding at the ears. All were full of courage and worked with a will; they were so begrimed with powder that they looked like negroes.

"Pass along the cartridges."

"More powder."

"A shell for number six."

"A wet wad for the hot-shot gun."

"Put out that pipe and don't light it again on peril of your life,"

Such were the directions and commands, issued like clockwork amid the confusion of battle. Our executive officer seemed to be in a dozen places at once.

This gives some faint notion of the scene passing behind our grim iron casement, which to the beholders without seemed a machine of destruction. Human hearts were beating and bleeding there. Human lives were being sacrificed. Pain, death, wounds, glory —that was the sum of it.

On the doomed ship *Cumberland* the battle raged with equal fury. The sanded deck was red and slippery with blood. Delirium seized the crew. They stripped to their trousers, kicked off their shoes, tied handkerchiefs about their heads, and fought and cheered as their ship sank beneath their feet. Then the order came, "All save who can." There was a scramble for the spar - deck and a rush overboard. The ship listed. The after pivot-gun broke loose and rushed down the decline like a furious animal, rolling over a man as it bounded overboard, leaving a mass of mangled flesh on deck.

We now turned to the *Congress,* which had tried to escape but had grounded, and the battle raged once more, broadside upon broadside, delivered at close range, the *Merrimac* working closer all the time with her bow pointed as if to ram the *Congress.* A shell from Lieutenant Wood's gun sped through their line of powder-passers, not only cutting down the men, but exploding the powder buckets in their hands, spreading death and destruction and setting fire to the ship.

At last came the order, "Cease firing."

"The *Congress* has surrendered," some one cried. " Look out of the port. See, she has run up white flags. The officers are waving their handkerchiefs."

At this several of the officers started to leave their posts and rush on deck,

THE "MERRIMAC" DRIVING THE "CONGRESS" FROM HER ANCHORAGE.

LIEUTENANT CATESBY AP R. JONES OF
THE "MERRIMAC."

THE MERRIMAC AND THE MONITOR

but Lieutenant Jones in his stentorian voice sang out: "Stand by your guns, and, lieutenants, be ready to resume firing at the word. See that your guns are well supplied with ammunition during the lull. Dr. Garnett, see how those poor fellows yonder are coming on. Mr. Littlepage, tell Paymaster Semple to have a care of the berth-deck and use every precaution against fire. Mr. Hasker, call away the cutter's crew and have them in readiness. Mr. Lindsay [to the carpenter], sound the well, examine the forehold, and report if you find anything wrong." Such was Catesby Ap. R. Jones, the executive officer of the *Merrimac.*

When it was fully evident that there was to be a suspension of hostilities, and these details had all been attended to, several of the officers went to stand beside Buchanan on the upper grating.

The whole scene was changed. A pall of black smoke hung about the ships and obscured the clean-cut outlines of the shore. Down the river were the three frigates *St. Lawrence, Roanoke,* and *Minnesota,* also enveloped in the clouds of battle that now and then reflected the crimson lightnings of the god of war. The masts of the *Cumberland* were protruding above the water. The *Congress* presented a terrible scene of carnage.

The gunboats *Beaufort* and *Raleigh* were signaled to take off the wounded and fire the ship. They were driven away by sharpshooters on shore, who suddenly turned their fire on us, notwithstanding the white flag of the *Congress.*

THE MERRIMAC AND THE MONITOR

Buchanan fell, severely wounded in the groin.

As he was being carried below he said to Executive Officer Jones: "Plug hot shot into her and don't leave her until she's afire. They must look after their own wounded, since they won't let us"—a characteristic command when it is remembered that his own brother, McKean Buchanan, was paymaster of the *Congress* and might have been numbered among the wounded.

We had kept two furnaces for the purpose of heating shot. They were rolled into the flames on a grating, rolled out into iron buckets, hoisted to the gun-deck, and rolled into the guns, which had been prepared with wads of wet hemp. Then the gun would be touched off quickly and the shot sent on its errand of destruction.

Leaving the *Congress* wrapped in sheets of flame, we made for the three other frigates. The *St. Lawrence* and *Roanoke* had run aground, but were pulled off by tugs and made their escape. The *Minnesota* was not so fortunate, but we drew twenty-three feet of water and could not get near enough to destroy her, while our guns could not be elevated owing to the narrow embrasures, and their range was only a mile; so we made for our moorings at Sewall's Point.

All the evening we stood on deck watching the brilliant display of the burning ship. Every part of her was on fire at the same time, the red-tongued flames running up shrouds, masts, and stays, and extending out to the

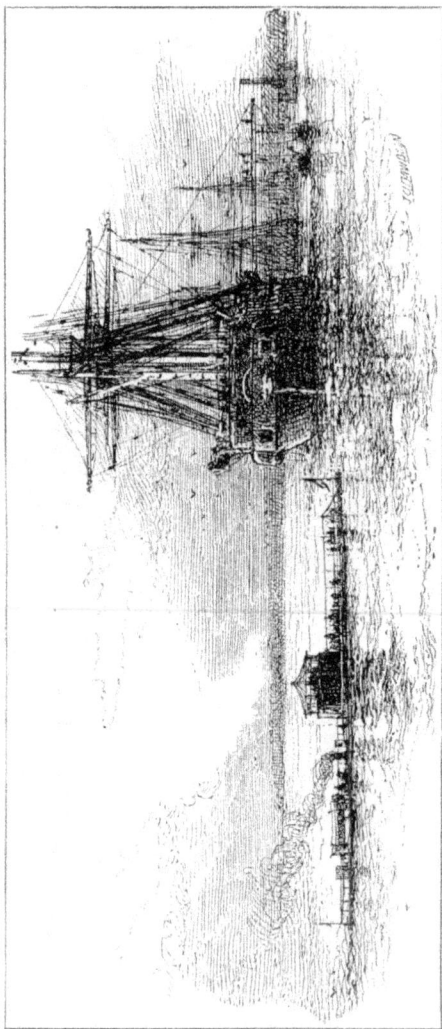

ARRIVAL OF THE "MONITOR" AT HAMPTON ROADS.

yard-arms. She stood in bold relief against the black background, lighting up the Roads and reflecting her lurid lights on the bosom of the now placid and hushed waters. Every now and then the flames would reach one of the loaded cannon and a shell would hiss at random through the darkness. About midnight came the grand finale. The magazines exploded, shooting up a huge column of firebrands hundreds of feet in the air, and then the burning hulk burst asunder and melted into the waters, while the calm night spread her sable mantle over Hampton Roads.

The *Monitor* arrived during the evening and anchored under the stern of the *Minnesota,* her lighter draught enabling her to do so without danger. To us the ensuing engagement was in

THE MERRIMAC AND THE MONITOR

the nature of a surprise. If we had known we were to meet her we would have at least been supplied with solid shot for our rifled guns. We might even have thought best to wait until our iron beak, lost in the side of the *Cumberland,* could be replaced. Buchanan was incapacitated by his wound, and the command devolved upon Lieutenant Jones.

We left our anchorage shortly before eight o'clock next morning and steamed across and up stream toward the *Minnesota,* thinking to make short work of her and soon return with her colors trailing under ours. We approached her slowly, feeling our way cautiously along the edge of the channel, when suddenly, to our astonishment, a black object that looked like the historic description, "a barrel -

48

head afloat with a cheese-box on top of it," moved slowly out from under the *Minnesota* and boldly confronted us. It must be confessed that both ships were queer-looking craft, as grotesque to the eyes of the men of '62 as they would appear to those of the present generation.

And now the great fight was on, a fight the like of which the world had never seen. With the battle of yesterday old methods had passed away, and with them the experience of a thousand years "of battle and of breeze" was brought to naught.

We hovered about each other in spirals, gradually contracting the circuits until we were within point-blank range, but our shell glanced from the *Monitor's* turret just as hers did from our sloping sides. For two hours the cannonade continued without perceptible damage to either of the combatants.

On our gun-deck all was bustle, smoke, grimy figures, and stern commands, while down in the engine and boiler rooms the sixteen furnaces were belching out fire and smoke, and the firemen standing in front of them, like so many gladiators, tugged away with devil's-claw and slice-bar, inducing by their exertions more and more intense combustion and heat. The noise of the cracking, roaring fires, escaping steam, and the loud and labored pulsations of the engines, together with the roar of battle above and the thud and vibration of the huge masses of iron which were hurled against us produced a scene and sound to be compared only with

ON THE GUN-DECK OF THE "MERRIMAC"

the poet's picture of the lower regions.

And then an accident occurred that threatened our utter destruction. We stuck fast aground on a sand-bar.

Our situation was critical. The *Monitor* could, at her leisure, come close up to us and yet be out of our reach, owing to our inability to deflect our guns. In she came and began to sound every chink in our armor —every one but that which was actually vulnerable, had she known it.

The coal consumption of the two days' fight had lightened our prow until our unprotected submerged deck was almost awash. The armor on our sides below the water-line had been extended but about three feet, owing to our hasty departure before the work was finished. Lightened as we were, these exposed portions rendered us no longer an ironclad, and the *Monitor* might have pierced us between wind and water had she depressed her guns.

Fearing that she might discover our vulnerable "heel of Achilles" we had to take all chances. We lashed down the safety valves, heaped quick-burning combustibles into the already raging fires, and brought the boilers to a pressure that would have been unsafe under ordinary circumstances. The propeller churned the mud and water furiously, but the ship did not stir. We piled on oiled cotton waste, splints of wood, anything that would burn faster than coal. It seemed impossible that the boilers could stand the pressure we were crowding upon them. Just as we were beginning to despair

THE MERRIMAC AND THE MONITOR

there was a perceptible movement, and the *Merrimac* slowly dragged herself off the shoal by main strength. We were saved.

Before our adversary saw that we were again afloat we made a dash for her, catching her quite unprepared, and tried to ram her, but our commander was dubious about the result, of a collision without our iron-shod beak, and gave the signal to reverse the engines long before we reached the *Monitor.* As a result I did not feel the slightest shock down in the engine-room, though we struck her fairly enough.

The carpenter reported that the effect was to spring a leak forward. Lieutenant Jones sent for me and asked me about it.

"It is impossible we can be making

53

much water," I replied, "for the skin of the vessel is plainly visible in the crank-pits."

A second time he sent for me and asked if we were making any water in the engine-room.

"With the two large Worthington pumps, besides the bilge injections, we could keep her afloat for hours, even with a ten-inch shell in her hull," I assured him, repeating that there was no water in the engine and boiler rooms.

We glided past, leaving the *Monitor* unscathed, but got between her and the *Minnesota* and opened fire on the latter. The *Monitor* gallantly rushed to her rescue, passing so close under our submerged stern that she almost snapped off our propeller. As she was passing, so near that we could have

THE MERRIMAC AND THE MONITOR

leaped aboard her, Lieutenant Wood trained the stem-gun on her when she was only twenty yards from its muzzle and delivered a rifle-pointed shell which dislodged the iron logs sheltering the *Monitor's* conning-tower, carrying away the steering-gear and signal apparatus, and blinding Captain Worden. It was a mistake to place the conning-tower so far from the turret and the vitals of the ship. Since that time it has been located over the turret. The *Monitor's* turret was a death-trap. It was only twenty feet in diameter, and every shot knocked off bolt-heads and sent them flying against the gunners. If one of them barely touched the side of the turret he would be stunned and momentarily paralyzed. Lieutenant Greene had been taken below in a dazed condition and never fully recovered from the effects. One of the port, shutters had been jammed, putting a gun out of commission, and there was nothing for the *Monitor* to do but to retreat and leave the *Minnesota* to her fate.

Captain Van Brunt, of the latter vessel, thought he was now doomed and was preparing to fire his ship when he saw the *Merrimac* also withdrawing toward Norfolk.

It was at this juncture that Lieutenant Jones had sent for me and said: "The pilots will not place us nearer to the *Minnesota* , and we cannot afford to run the risk of getting aground again. I'm going to haul off under the guns of Sewall's Point and renew the attack on the rise of the tide. Bank your fires and make any necessary adjustments to the machinery, but be prepared to start up again later in the afternoon."

I went below to comply with his instructions, and later was astonished to hear cheering. Rushing on deck, I found we were passing Craney Island on our way to Norfolk, and were being cheered by the soldiers of the battery.

Our captain had consulted with some of his lieutenants. He explained afterward that as the *Monitor* had proved herself so formidable an adversary he had thought best to get a supply of solid shot, have the prow replaced, the port shutters put on, the armor belt extended below water, and the guns whose muzzles had been shot away replaced, and then renew the engagement with every chance of victory. I remember feeling as though a wet blanket had been thrown over me. His reasoning was doubtless good, but it ignored the moral effect of leaving the Roads without forcing the *Minnesota* to surrender.

As the *Merrimac* passed up the river, trailing the ensign of the *Congress* under the stars and bars, she received a tremendous ovation from the crowds that lined the shores, while hundreds of small boats, gay with flags and bunting, converted our course into a triumphal procession.

We went into dry-dock that very afternoon, and in about three weeks were ready to renew the battle upon more advantageous terms, but the *Monitor,* though reinforced by two other ironclads, the *Galena* and the *Naugatuck,* and every available vessel

58

COMMANDERS OF THE "VIRGINIA" (OR "MERRIMAC").

Franklin Buchanan, Admiral, C.S.N   Josiah Tattnall, Commodore, C.S.N

of the United States navy, was under orders from Washington to refuse our challenge and bottle us up in the Roads. This strategy filled us with rage and dismay, but it proved very effective.

Our new commander, Commodore Josiah Tatnall, was burning to distinguish himself, but he was under orders not to risk the destruction or capture of the *Merrimac* by leaving the Roads, as General Huger's division at Norfolk would then be at the mercy of the Federal fleet. Week after week was passing and with it his golden opportunity. At last we went to Richmond and pressed a plan for a sortie upon the President. He returned one afternoon and ordered every one aboard. That night we slipped down the Roads and were soon passing Fort Monroe on our way out into the Chesapeake.

Presently our army signal officer began waving his lantern communicating with our distant batteries, and then told the result to Officer Jones, who reported to Tatnall. "We have been ordered to return, sir," he said.

Tatnall was viewing the dim outlines of the fort through his glass and pretended not to hear.

"The order is peremptory," repeated Jones.

Tatnall hesitated. He was of half a mind to disobey. "Old Huger has outwitted me," he muttered. "Do what you please. I leave you in command. I'm going to bed," and he went below in a high dudgeon. Tatnall was a striking-looking man, standing over six feet, with florid complexion, deep-sunken blue eyes, and a protruding under lip. That he did not have a chance to fight was no fault of his.

Our life on board for the weeks that followed was far from comfortable. We were within sight of the enemy, and at every movement of the opposing fleet it was "clear away for action." Steam was kept up continually. Our cabins were without air ports and no ray of light even penetrated the ward-rooms. There was nowhere to walk but on the upper grating—a modern prison is far more comfortable. Sometimes the sailors waded on the submerged deck, giving rise to the superstition among the darkies that they were the crew of the "debble ship" with power to walk on the water.

THE MERRIMAC AND THE MONITOR

Norfolk was now being evacuated and we were covering Huger's retreat. When this was effected we were to receive the signal and to make our own way up the James. Norfolk was in Federal hands, and Huger had disappeared without signaling us, when our pilots informed us that Harrison's Bar, which we must cross, drew only eighteen feet of water. Under their advice, on the night of May 11th we lightened ship by throwing overboard all our coal and ballast, thus raising our unprotected decks above water. At last all was ready —and then we found that the wind which had been blowing down-stream all day had swept the water off the bar. When morning dawned the Federal fleet must discover our defenseless condition, and defeat and capture were certain, for we were now no longer an ironclad.

It was decided to abandon the vessel and set her on fire. We took the *Merrimac* to the bight of Craney Island, and about midnight the work of disembarking the crew began. We had but two boats, and it was sunrise before our three hundred and fifty men were all ashore. Cotton waste and trains of powder were strewn about the deck, and Executive Officer Jones, who was the last to leave the ship, applied the slow match. Then we marched silently through the woods to join Huger, fifteen miles away at Suffolk.

Still unconquered, we hauled down our drooping colors, their laurels all fresh and green, with mingled pride and grief, gave her to the flames, and set the lambent fires roaring about the shotted guns. The slow match, the magazine, and that last, deep, low, sullen, mournful boom told our people, now far away on the march, that their gallant ship was no more.

Photo # NH 58724   Destruction of CSS Virginia (ex-USS Merrimack). Engraving from "Harper's Weekly"

DESTRUCTION OF THE CONFEDERATE IRONCLAD "MERRIMACK," BLOWN UP BY HER COMMANDER, MAY 11th, 1862.

FROM A SKETCH TAKEN FROM CRANEY ISLAND.

THE LAST OF THE MONITOR

III

THE LAST OF THE MONITOR

By an eye-witness, Rear-Admiral E. W. Watson, U. S. N.

ON the 29th of December, 1862, nine months after her memorable combat with the *Merrimac,* the *Monitor,* Commander John P. Bankhead, left Hampton Roads in tow of the *Rhode Island,* commanded by Captain Stephen Decatur Trenchard, for Beaufort, North Carolina. The weather at the time of starting looked favorable for the trip, but on the following day, when nearing Cape Hatteras, the wind came out from the southeast and gradually freshened until by evening it was blowing a moderate gale, with a tolerably heavy sea running. It was soon seen that the *Monitor* was making heavy weather of it, and the engines were slowed down, but the course was still kept head to the wind and sea.

This was a mistake, for experience later on in towing other vessels of her class proved that the safest way to handle them in heavy weather was to let them lie in the trough of the sea, when the waves would wash over their decks and the roll would not be excessive. The *Monitor* was closely watched, all on board the *Rhode Island* feeling anxious for her safety. Toward the end of the first watch—between 8 P.M. and midnight—the signal of distress, a red lan-

THE LAST OF THE MONITOR

tern, was hoisted on the *Monitor*, and, unknown to those on the *Rhode Island*, the hawser was cut and the anchor of the *Monitor* let go.

The *Rhode Island* immediately stopped her engine, and three boats were called away with an officer in charge of each, and were sent to take off the *Monitor's* people. With the heavy sea running it was a difficult matter to go alongside of her, and the first boat to reach her was thrown by a wave upon the deck and a hole stove in her. The next wave washed the boat off, and with considerable difficulty she took on board as many of the men as in her leaky condition could make the return trip safely.

When the boats came alongside of the *Monitor*, her captain and executive officer went upon the deck and,

THE LAST OF THE MONITOR

clinging to the life-lines with the waves washing over them, called to the crew to come down from the turret and get into the boats, which they were reluctant to do at first. Some were able to jump into the boats, and some landed in the water and were hauled in. Seeing an old quartermaster with a large bundle under his arm, the executive officer, thinking that it was his clothes-bag, told him that that was no time to be trying to save his effects. He said nothing, but threw it into the boat. When the bundle was passed up over the side of the *Rhode Island* it proved to be a little messenger-boy—probably the smallest and youngest one in the service. The three boats were finally loaded and made their way back to the ship.

SINKING OF THE "MONITOR."

THE LAST OF THE MONITOR

In the mean while the *Rhode Island,* in backing her engines, had fouled the hawser with her port paddle-wheel, and being directly to windward of the *Monitor,* with her engines helpless, drifted down upon her. It looked at one time as if she would strike the bow of the *Monitor,* but, fortunately, she just missed it, and, scraping along her side, drifted off to leeward.

Another boat was sent to bring off the remainder of the *Monitor's* crew, but, being to leeward now, she could make only slow headway against the seas, and before she got to her the men saw the *Monitor's* light disappear, and knew that she had gone down. The hawser having finally been cleared from the *Rhode Island's* wheel, she steamed around searching for the boat, sending up rockets and burning blue lights to show her position. When the day dawned nothing could be seen. After hailing a passing government vessel and telling them to search for the boat, the *Rhode Island* steamed with all speed for Fortress Monroe to report the loss.

When the survivors of the ill-fated vessel were mustered on the deck of the *Rhode Island,* four officers and twelve men were found missing, all of them probably buried in an iron coffin in a watery grave about fifty miles to the southward and eastward of Cape Hatteras Light.

The missing boat and crew of the *Rhode Island* were found by that vessel a week later safe in Beaufort,

THE LAST OF THE MONITOR

North Carolina. They had been picked up by a schooner and taken into that port. The officer in charge of the boat reported that in the early morning he had sighted a schooner standing toward them, and had hoisted a black silk handkerchief belonging to one of the crew on an oar as a signal of distress, but the people in the schooner, evidently thinking them pirates who had come out of some one of the inlets of the coast, turned tail and scudded away from them. A second schooner, coming along soon after, was more hospitable and took them aboard.

THE END